RETHINK EVERYTHING

KYLE DRAPER

Cover by Ric Dominic Zarate
Illustrations by Justine Karl Zarate
Layout by Princess Hannah Arsenio

RETHINK
EVERYTHING
YOU "KNOW" ABOUT SOCIAL MEDIA

KYLE DRAPER

Acknowledgements

I am so grateful for each member of our team that has played a role in this book. Without each and every one of you, this book remains a fraction of what it was capable of becoming. Thank you for your hard work and commitment to serving people at the highest level! Each one of you played a special role in this process. *You're the best!*

Aiko Perez
Chenani Micah Valor
Gwynda Miranda
Holly Bormann
Janine Ignes
Jean Ann Knox
Jerson Bandola
Justine Karl Zarate
Krystle Hays-Urbina
Kyla Nacario
Maky Castillo
Nicole Marzan
Princess Hannah Arsenio
Raymond Marzan
Ric Dominic Zarate
Stephanie Qualls

CONTENTS

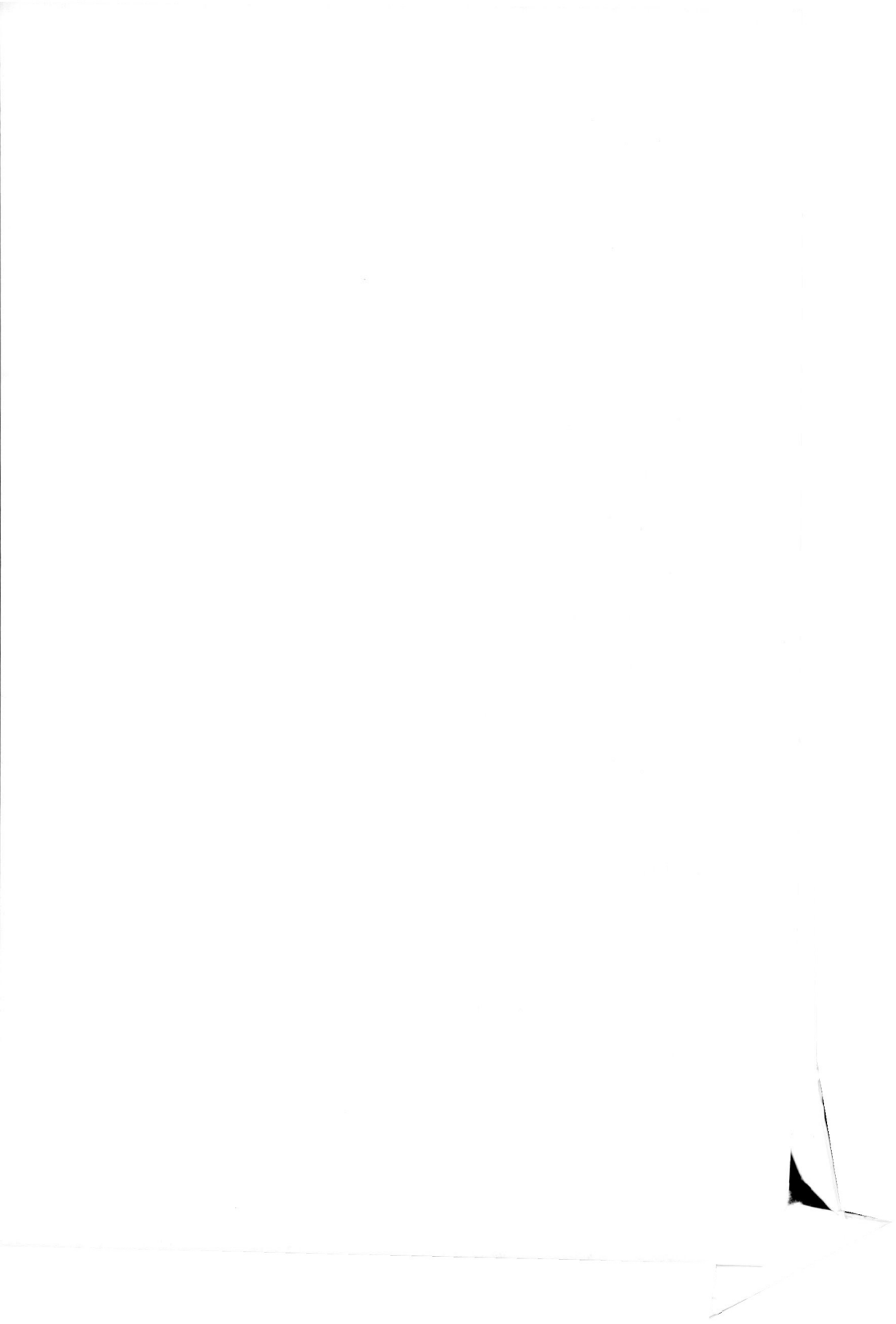

Foreword

Social Media can be polarizing. Social Media can also be life-changing... in a good way!

The 2009 book *"Crush It"* by Gary Vaynerchuk challenged me to start doing video. Executive Coaches weren't doing much of that then, and I didn't do a very good job of it. *Think I'm kidding? Here's my second video:*

Video and Social Media changed the trajectory of my career. So many of the principles that Kyle is about to introduce you to are lessons I learned painfully along the way.

Once I started turning on the camera and posting video, a funny thing happened; people I hadn't met started to say "I feel like I know you." Kyle mentions this specifically, and I'm here to tell you that this is game-changing.

The other thing I've always thought about Social Media, but have never said is something Kyle calls out here as well; Social Media is what you make of it. If you want to find angry polarizing people and posts - you won't have to look far. If, on the other hand, you're like me and are focused on the best in people, goodness and possibility—you'll find that, too.

Once... ONE TIME, years ago, I posted something political and inadvertently started an angry dialogue that I realized I just needed to delete. That has been my only negative experience with Social Media (other than catfishers stealing my images and preying on unsuspecting widows).

Social Media, as you are about to learn, is all about what you make of it. So make something wonderful!

Coach Bill Hart

INTRODUCTION

As I begin to write this book, I'm sitting outside my room at a resort in Cancun.

If I'm being honest (which I hate when people say), the reason I'm not asleep right now is because our room is too hot! Ha. So…instead of laying in a bed sweating while my beautiful wife sleeps, here we are.

Hi, I'm Kyle. I don't really know how I got here, but *I'm here*.

I spent almost 9 years in my 20's as a youth pastor in Plano, TX. Then, I left church ministry to start a roofing company with my dad and my brother. (I know, this is super weird, you're right, it is, but just hear me out) We moved to a state where I knew no one, and my journey with social media began.

The reason all of this matters is that some people hear me talk about social media and all of a sudden, they see it as their magic bullet. Guess what? It's not.

You see, social media is a tool. It's the most powerful tool that you have available to you…but it is useless on its own.

So, please don't read this book and think that you're going to do social media an hour a day and all of a sudden your business is going to explode…that's not how this works.

When you're out in your city meeting people; when you're showing up in people's lives and you add your social media on top of that type of effort, it gets magical.

Don't believe me, allow me to explain…

A GOOD TOOL

IMPROVES THE WAY YOU <u>WORK</u>

A GREAT TOOL

IMPROVES THE WAY YOU <u>THINK</u>

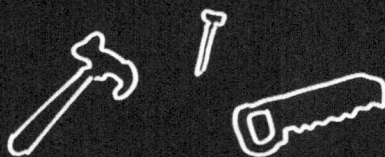

~ JEFF DUNTEMANN

It's 2013…we are living in Oklahoma City, I'm now a roofer, and I don't know anyone.

I start networking and meeting new people. While this is happening, I'm also dabbling in social media. I'm learning how to post, what to post, and who to post to.

Around this time Facebook Live becomes a thing… so I start going live from rooftops and just trying stuff. Zero plan, no organization, just trying to help people.

I also started friending REALTORS® on Facebook. Why? Because we started offering them free roof inspections before closings so the roof didn't hold them up.

And I kid you not…I started walking into events and people would go, "Wait, do I know you? Aren't you that guy?" I'd start laughing and say, "Yea, I'm the Facebook guy."

Don't miss this…they knew my son's name. They knew who Lana (my wife) was. It was wild!

This went on for months…

Friending people on Facebook.
Showing up in their DM's (direct messages).
Adding value.
Trying my best to be helpful.
Videos about roofing and other parts of my life.

NOTHING happened… until it did!

Small Disciplines repeated
with consistency every day
lead to great achievements
gained slowly over time.

-JOHN C. MAXWELL

The first hail storm (or sky diamonds, as roofers call them)
came through Oklahoma City since we'd lived there and

something CRAZY happened!

While every other roofer was out knocking on doors, I received almost 100 phone calls, text messages, comments on posts, and direct messages.

I was blown away. How did this happen? I didn't even know what I was doing. I had only been in roofing for a few months. But RELATIONSHIPS trump EVERYTHING!

That was the day that I realized that there is a greater power and authority that can come through social media if, and only if, we are willing to Rethink Everything.

In this book, I'm taking all the things that I learned on accident and I'm going to give it to you with great purpose.

But quickly, here's who this book IS NOT for...

If you don't care about serving people,
this book is not for you.
If you don't see a deeper purpose in your life other than making money, *this book is not for you.*
If you're not willing to play the long game,
this book is not for you.
If you have a longer list of what you won't do on social media than what you will do, *this book is not for you.*

BUT...

If you are willing to try anything, this book is for you. If what you've been currently doing isn't moving the needle, this book is for you.

If you're frustrated with your current social medial strategy...

This book is for you!

Welcome to RETHINK EVERYTHING!

This is BIGGER
than social media.

Are you ready to

RETHINK EVERYTHING?

KIND OF

CHAPTER 1:

Just kidding, it's not chapter one, I forgot one super important part…

The way you are currently doing social media sucks! (Maybe you are part of the small minority who does it right, but most likely you're not).

Why can I say this?

Because for many of you, you're a walking billboard for your business.

You post so selfishly. It's all about what's in this for you. Not, what serves the people you want to attract.

This has to change. If this book is going to work for you, you have to be able to admit that the current way isn't working. And be honest with yourself…it's never worked.

Posting about your products. Posting about how you love referrals. Posting your sales numbers each month. Yuck! I start dry heaving just thinking about how awful of a look this is.

It's time to BE BETTER. It's time to realize what Zig Ziglar has always said…

"You will have everything you want in life if you will just help other people get what they want."

This is the power! Use social media to be social and help others get what they want out of this thing we call life! That's my secret! Now, I hope to give you more tips than this over the course of this book…but that is the message in a nutshell!

Remove your selfish nature from your social media efforts and watch it skyrocket for you!

Last thing…throughout the book you'll see QR codes. I'll use them to tell a story or go deeper with a certain topic. You know what to do…scan those things and enjoy! :)

Ok, now we can jump into chapter one.

You will have everything
you want in life,
if you will just help
other people get what
they want.
~a

-ZIG ZIGLAR

CHAPTER 1:
Social Proof

If you're super legit (at business) in real life, but you look like you suck online...the perception is...YOU SUCK.

I know, it's a painful sentence to read, but the pain doesn't make it less true.

20 years ago, you just had to be good at your job. Outside of that, no one cared.

It's 2023, everything is different. Data is too available to us. We sleep with a device next to our head that can tell us anything that we'll ever want to know.

So, when your friend tells their friend about how great you are...they don't call you. They do what? They look you up!

This means if your friend tells them how amazing you are, how many awards you've won, and how many years you've been doing it...all of that goes away the moment they Google you and they can't find anything about you that holds any sort of value.

If you've refused to do any other platform than Facebook, the first page of Google will hardly be about you. If you haven't invested in creating videos so they can see your personality, experience your sense of humor or passion, and maybe even see how old your kids are...

You look like the opposite of all the nice things your friend told them about you.

Now, together, you and I, let's just say it...THIS IS NOT FAIR! You're right, it's not fair. But fair or not, perception matters more than reality.

Too many people have been sitting around complaining about how unfair the game is now instead of just getting in the game and learning as they go.

We now trust strangers more than our closest friends. Period. You have to rethink what social proof is and how it's killing your ability to get referral business and even convert online leads at a much higher level.

Strangers > Friends

Exercise: Go to Google or any social media platform and look yourself up. Are you impressed with what you see? If you didn't know you, would you hire yourself based on what the internet shows you about yourself? Again, be honest! This doesn't work if you aren't willing to do the exercise.

To-Do: Now, let's fix it! You know how you don't want Tiktok, or you didn't know how to use YouTube? Well, can we begin to see this differently? If someone Googles you, you want as many places as possible to pop up. You want your Facebook, Instagram, Tiktok, LinkedIn, YouTube, Twitter, and maybe even a podcast to show up. You don't have to pay attention to all these places, just have a presence there. You have to pass the EYE TEST! People are looking to have their friend's opinions of you validated. They may not even click on all the links, but if you look legit when they pull you up, they are going to call! This is why this is so important! This exercise alone will be a "game-changer" for you!

CHAPTER 2:
The Reason You Don't Do More

Video is the hardest thing we will ever do on social media because it is the most truth-telling mirror we will ever look into.

It forces us to come face-to-face with our flaws, our history, our insecurities, and our secrets.

We could talk about getting over the way you look or how your voice sounds, we could even talk through content strategies because you claim to not know what to talk about, but the real reason isn't any of those excuses.

The reason you don't do more video, or video at all for that matter, is because of your ego.

If you can't figure out how to put your ego aside on social media, it will eat your lunch every single day.

If you don't get enough views,
your ego will suffer.

If you don't get followers fast enough,
your ego will suffer.

If you don't get enough engagement,
your ego will suffer.

If you need to serve your ego, your people will suffer.

GIVE THEM WHAT THEY NEED,

NOT WHAT YOU WANT!

– KYLE DRAPER

So, how do we overcome ego? You have to care more about helping others than you do about looking stupid. That's it…

That's one of my superpowers. I genuinely want to help others succeed so badly, I will go to any lengths necessary to accomplish that. Even having my ego bruised when the video that I thought would crush only got 100 views.

You have the desire to serve people right now. The moment you allow that heart to be more powerful than what people think about you, it's game on!

As I've developed this within myself, here are a couple of strategies I'd love to talk through together.

#1 - Assume The Best In Others.

I've realized that when I assume the worst in others, I also start believing that others assume the worst in me. It jacks with my headspace. It causes me to start thinking weirdly. And quite frankly, when I assume the worst in others, I'm just frustrated and ticked off all the time. That doesn't make for the best environment for you to show up in front of the camera. As you start assuming the best in others, watch it allow you to find yourself in front of the camera more often.

#2 - Be Curious, Not Judgemental.

Now, I believe this is a Walt Witman quote…but my favorite story of this quote being used is from my favorite show, Ted Lasso. So, instead of trying to tell you the story, scan this QR code and watch it real quick.

This quote impacts me in two ways…first, if you want to make the right content, you better get curious about the people you serve. If you don't know them, you'll never make content that attracts them. Secondly, If you're constantly judging others, you're going to feel judged. That's going to cause you to want to hide instead of being out in the forefront. Be a better human! That's the underlying theme of this book.

As we bring this chapter to a close, I want you to think about this.

Your opinion doesn't make you money! Look at who you sell to…it's NOT YOU! It's others. Let their opinion matter the most.

The content game changed for me when I quit asking my wife to watch my videos. No one had the ability to be more critical than her. So she would ask questions about why I said that or did something, I'd get discouraged, then I wouldn't post the video. At the moment I didn't see it, but I was self-sabotaging myself.

The moment I realized that my wife wasn't my ideal client, I then realized her opinion then, doesn't matter. (Sidebar…her opinion matters THE MOST for everything else in my life!) It changed my ability to crank out content.

If I don't like it, who cares! If Lana doesn't like it, who cares! If my ideal clients like it, it's golden!

Your perspective has to change on this! You are locked in your own prison and what's crazy…you're holding the key!

I said it earlier…if you can't find that place in your spirit where you can say, "I love serving people more than I care about looking stupid," you will struggle.

So, look around you…

Do you see people in your industry with bigger businesses than you, but care about people less than you do? Do you see people in your industry with more opportunities coming their way, but selfish motives? Do something about it! Go serve people! Right now.

Exercise: Write down as many questions as you can that you've been asked by friends, family, or clients about your industry.

To-Do: Go record your "Origin Story" video. Tell people who you are. I'll explain more when you scan the QR code.

> "Everything that needs to be said has already been said, but, since no one was listening, everything must be said again."
>
> ~))

CHAPTER 3:
Everything Has Already Been Said

French writer, Andre Gide, said, "Everything that needs to be said has already been said, but, since no one was listening, everything must be said again."

I love this quote for one BIG reason!

Say it AGAIN! Say it AGAIN! Say it AGAIN!

As you start to put out more content, if you're not careful, you'll instantly overwhelm yourself with the need to be creative and convince yourself that you need to put out something that no one else is doing. It's not possible though…

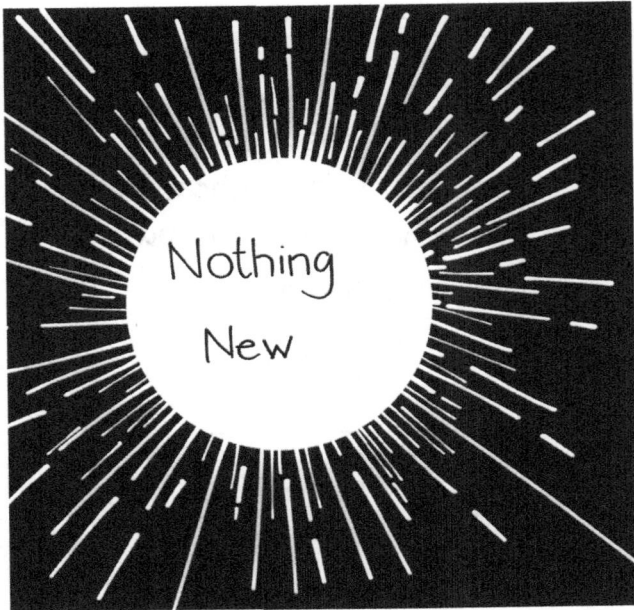

2000 years ago the Bible said in Ecclesiastes, "there is nothing new under the sun," and that was before the internet! Before social media. If people 2000 years ago were already overthinking their creativity and their need to always be different...how much worse is it now?

So, when it comes to content, don't overthink it. Understand the needs of your people, accept you for yourself, and just keep cranking through your ideas.

I've heard it said, "your best idea is your next idea."

Just keep going. And since I already know you're going to struggle (because we all do)…here are four ways to ensure you always have something of value to talk about.

#1 - Write down every question you've been asked about your profession and/or business.

If someone is asking you, others are thinking it. Give them what you already know they want. This should be your main strategy for building out your YouTube channel. Commonly asked questions. Very simple and straightforward. If you're funny, be funny. If you're not, don't try to be. Be yourself and start knocking these out. I'd shoot for one or two a week. If you can manage one, that's 52 videos on your channel after one year. That's huge!

#2 - Ask yourself, "what I am surprised that people don't already know?"

When you're in conversation with people and they stop you and ask for a deeper explanation, that should trigger an alarm in your head that says, make this into a video! Here's the reason this is so powerful… if you can begin predicting the questions people are already going to have and then have a place for people to watch those videos, they will think you're a mind reader. That will cause them to instantly think you're more qualified and capable than others. It's a powerful, powerful, tool.

#3 - Use www.AnswerThePublic.com

This website is crazy! You can type in any word or phrase and it will show you all the different ways that word or phrase is being used in a Google search. It's wild! The last time I used it, it gave me 384 search results to help me deep dive into content for one subject matter. If you use this tool, you'll never wonder what to talk about again. PS - You get one free search a day. Don't search for something stupid first, ha.

#4 - Go to YouTube, type in your industry in the search, go to competitors' channels and just look at what they are titling their videos.

This isn't rocket science. There's a good chance that if your competitors are talking about it on the internet, maybe you should be too. Their titles will give you everything you need to know about what you may not be thinking about talking through. Don't watch their videos and psyche yourself out, just use their titles to come up with your next video. Keep it simple.

My favorite way to feel empowered to say what's already been said is to regurgitate what I'm learning.

CELEBRATE

&

COPY

-Austin Kleon

If you're in sales and/or leadership and you are not already passionate about personal development, you should be. I use my personal development to make content constantly. (As I write this, I'm in the middle of 30 Days of Leadership. It's a video a day for 30 days. It's grueling, but gets you in the habit of recording videos quickly.)

When I read something that resonates with me, I don't just underline it and apply it, I also love to talk about it. I will jump on camera right at that moment (if you don't, you'll lose the passion for the idea later), give credit to the author, even flash the book on camera, then talk through it.

Here's what's crazy, nobody gives credit to the author, they give credit to me as the one who delivered the message. They don't tag the author on social media when they talk about it, they tag me. It's the weirdest thing.

Also, think about this...when one of your people buys a book that you recommend, who do you think they think about every time they see that book sitting on their desk or on their bookshelf? YOU!

If you do this right, you'll be playing social media chess while others are stuck playing checkers. This is a true game-changer!

My favorite book is called "Steal Like An Artist" by Austin Kleon. I talk about it all the time. I also get tagged in selfies of people holding the book. In their post, they aren't thanking Austin, they thank me. This works over and over again!

The last thing to be mindful of is this…if your ego gets in the way, you won't do this strategy. You'll convince yourself that you're a loser because you aren't coming up with all new content that no one has seen before. Then you'll start thinking about what you can do that will go viral. Remember, a desire to go viral serves one person, you. Be intentional. Be okay with only getting a couple of hundred views by the right people. That's where the money is made!

Exercise: Make a list of your favorite books/authors, podcasts, and/or YouTube channels.

To-Do: Pick a quote from one of your favorite books or authors and do a video about it. Then begin doing this one to two times a month.

WHEN TRUST IS
ESTABLISHED,

EVERYTHING WILL
GO WELL FOR YOU.

BUT NOT JUST
ONCE,

OVER AND OVER
AGAIN!

CHAPTER 4:
Love People

If you haven't told someone recently that your product/service isn't for them or that they're not ready, you may not love people the way you think you do. Hear me out…

There's no way that every single human on the planet is right for your product or service. You are always going to run into people that aren't the right fit for what you offer. If you're not willing to say no to them because all you care about is the sale, you don't love people the way you should.

For most salespeople, if we aren't careful, the first thing to go is our genuine love for people. We begin to value money over relationships. We turn everything into a numbers game. We accept a certain percentage of success and then we just burn through people trying to find the yes. Then we rinse and repeat.

If you are selling $10 trinkets to people all over the planet, that's a fine strategy. But if you are local and hope to be a referral-heavy business, don't bring that strategy to the table unless you want to ruin every relationship you have.

I love to tell the rooms of people I speak to that I don't want their business. And I mean it. I tell them that they can only give me their money once, but their friends can give me quite a bit more. So, my number one goal when talking to people is to get them to trust me. That's it.

When trust is established, everything will go well for you. But not just once, over and over again!

I get so many organic opportunities because I simply serve people well.

Here are the ways I've accomplished this…

#1 - Treat others as better than yourself.

The Apostle Paul said, "Be humble, treating others as better than yourselves." I love that verse! Humility is such a hard thing to grasp. The minute you think you've achieved it, you quit working on it and it's the first thing to go away and pride shows up in its place. What I've found that works is regularly asking myself why I do what I do. Am I doing it for the accolades of others and my own personal gain or am I doing it to serve the needs of others?

#2 - consider their story.

We don't know what people are going through. We could be experiencing them for the first time in their worst moment. Then we create this narrative in our head of what we think about them and/or what we think they need. We must be careful not to judge someone so quickly. Someone unassuming may be the relationship you need that leads you to your biggest opportunity. Let's be careful not to write people off so quickly

#3 - Allow yourself to be taken advantage of.

A long time ago I heard someone say they were just thankful to have something worth taking advantage of. When I heard that, I thought, wow, that's powerful. What a mindset shift. Instead of being stingy and holding back, I'm just going to give unapologetically. When you start picking and choosing who you're willing to help, you tend to start helping those that can help you the most and stop helping those who need the most help. Give it all away. People will still pay you for it if it's good enough! Because they don't just want the tips, they want proximity to you, they want processes, they want details. Keep giving!

#4 - Be a connector.

When I got into roofing I was coached by Michael Maher. He wrote the best-selling book, "Seven Levels of Communication." One of his strategies was to be the reason people know each other. So, I would spend time asking others who they needed to know next in their business, then I'd make it happen. What I found was that just asking others that question made them feel like they owed you. Ha. But as I asked them more, I would start getting things like, I would love to know another insurance agent or builder. Then, boom, I'd make the intro! Now, the only reason those people know each other is because of me. It works every time!

As I wrap up this chapter, think about this...our world sucks. Everything under the sun seems to divide us more than it unites us. So, I work my butt off to just be the guy that brings light to every room I walk into. I want people to say, I just love being around Kyle. I feel better about myself when Kyle is around. The mood is lighter when Kyle is around. I feel like I can tell Kyle the good things that happen in my life because he'll genuinely celebrate with me.

If your biggest goal is to lighten the burden of those around you, bring light to dark places, and to love people whether they're lovable or not, your business and life will never stop getting better.

Exercise: Make a short list of who you'd like to know that you don't know yet.

To-Do: Reach out to them as a connector. Ask them who they'd like to know and then figure out how to make an introduction. You do this enough times, you'll start feeling the reciprocation of all that giving.

"SOME DO,
OTHERS WILL,
AND THE
REST DON'T
MATTER."

KYLE DRAPER

CHAPTER 5:
Accept Your Issues

If you spend your time comparing yourself to others, you'll never measure up.

If you never measure up, you'll feel completely inadequate on social media.

We have to fix this now. I mean, right now.

What is it?

What is it that causes us to so easily think we are "less than" compared to other people?

It's so easy.

Being confident is hard, but doggin' ourselves is simple.

Here's the fix…

I don't think it starts with gaining confidence…I think it starts with recognizing that everyone is just as screwed up as you.

We are so quick to show so much grace to others, yet offer zero to ourselves.

I know, there are a million self-help books out there, so if this were that easy, you'd have done it already.

But, what the heck? Let's try!

Here are some of the daily practices that help me. Again, they aren't perfect, but they are effective.

#1 - Someone out there envies your life.
Have you ever thought about that? You have people around you that say, "Must be nice…" That is reality. Wanting the gifts of others isn't a one-way street.

There are people out there right now jealous of who you are. Now, don't let this go to your head...but let it give you some perspective. You're a big deal! Others see it in you, but none of that matters until you believe it for yourself.

#2 - You're more relatable the more imperfect you are.

We often try to appear to be perfect on social media... even though perfection is a quality we dislike in other people. A great tool to use in your video content is self-deprecating humor. If you can poke fun at yourself on camera and get people laughing...you're not only relatable but will instantly improve your presence. You'll feel lighter. You'll be less worried about messing up. Because messing up is what relatable people do. Be relatable...

#3 - Be a student, not an expert.

Most people want to only talk about what they think they are the experts of on social media. So, for many, you convince yourself you don't have anything to say because deep down, you're not the expert on anything yet. Let's flip this! Be the passionate student bringing others on the journey. It works just as well as being the expert, but it opens your options up to literally anything. This is the most freeing way to create content.

Finally, the most basic, but important part.

Very few people like what they look like, enjoy hearing themselves talk, or regularly know what to talk about on social media.

So guess what?

You look like WHAT YOU LOOK LIKE!
There, I said it!

If you're "older," you're older.

If you're overweight, you're overweight.

If you have a high-pitched voice, you have a high-pitched voice.

But you know what?

You still go to coffee with people.

Y'all still do double dates.

You don't allow those things to keep you from being physically around people...video and social media are no different. The only person being fooled is you.

It is time for that mindset to change!

Exercise: Make a list of what you're good at. Don't stop at less than 7.

To-Do: Now that you have this list, how can your list help your social media presence?

"Listen with curiosity. Speak with honesty. Act with integrity. The greatest problem with communication is we don't listen to understand. We listen to reply. When we listen with curiosity, we don't listen with the intent to reply. We listen for what's behind the words."

— Roy T. Bennett,
   The Light in the Heart

CHAPTER 6:
Actually Listen

Do you remember when we were kids and we would play "Double Dutch" on the playground?

Since I was always the big kid, I typically chose to be on the end. I was a great jump rope handler, not so much of a jumper...

The jumper had to be quick, they had to have fast feet, and they had to be able to predict when the precise moment was coming for them to jump in.

Your ability to anticipate when to jump in is a killer skill set for jumping rope...but when we start using that skill set while someone else is talking, it's no longer a good thing.

For most people, they treat conversations with others like double dutch...

We will pretend to listen to the other person while really waiting for our turn to talk. The moment we feel them take a breath...BOOM! We pounce in with whatever it is that we want to say.

When we don't actually listen, we don't truly hear them...we miss their questions, their concerns, and their struggles...This is a big reason why we struggle with content.

Future, current, and past clients ask you questions all the time, but you still don't know what to talk about on social media. Why? Because you aren't ACTUALLY LISTENING, you are waiting to talk.

As experts in our field, if we aren't careful, we will assume we know what's best for someone and convince ourselves that we have the solutions. It's just a matter of hearing them out long enough to interject with infinite wisdom.

Do you want to actually listen?

Let's talk about a few strategies to instantly take you from pretending to listen to actually listening…

#1 - Pull out a pen and paper.

No matter who you're talking to…the moment y'all sit down, pull out a pen and paper. Then explain to them that they are going to say really important things and you don't want to miss them, so you make sure to write them down. They will be so impressed by that, you'll start earning their trust before y'all even get into the conversation. YOUR NOTES become your FUTURE CONTENT.

#2 - Ask a lot of questions.

Asking questions guarantees that we'll talk less. Asking questions shows people that you care more about them than yourself. Asking questions gives you extra opportunities to listen and write. If you don't naturally ask questions, you need to get more inquisitive.

Albert Einstein said, "I have no special talents. I am only passionately curious."

Do people fascinate you or frustrate you? How you answer that question will determine if you are a good listener or not.

#3 - Put your phone away.

When you are in conversations with people, you instantly let them know that they don't matter when your phone lights up and you look at it. So, if you can, put it completely away or at least turn it face down so it's not lighting up the entire meeting. We live so distractedly, this is our greatest adversary. If you'll remove distractions, you'll instantly listen more intently.

My daughter, who's eight, loves to get right in my face and say, "Dad, look at me, you're not listening." I hate when she does it because it reminds me of how good I am at listening at work but I don't give my family the attention they deserve.

Why does this matter? Because my eight-year-old can tell and so can the potential clients you meet. We all have room for improvement. Let's get committed to it!

Exercise: Make a list of 5 questions that you think will spur conversation with people. Do your best to pick questions that are truly about them, not questions that have an agenda attached to them.

To-Do: At your next appointment, use one or all of these questions, then record a video talking about what you discovered. Why? Because as you grow, your people need to grow too. Help them. They'll be thankful to you forever.

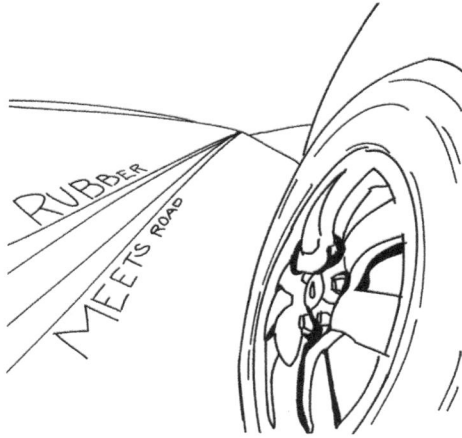

CHAPTER 7:
Are You Trustworthy?

Social Media has become a weird place…

It's no longer very social and mostly just salesy.

Though this sucks and is super annoying, the beauty of this is that if you'll do it differently, you have an easier opportunity to win.

When I am about to post on social media, I ask myself one question…

Does what I am about to post cause someone to trust me more or less?

That's it.

I want to give you a mid-chapter exercise instead of at the end...

Exercise: Go look at your social media, start scrolling, pretend you don't know yourself, and then begin to decide if you would trust this person or not.

Was this a fun exercise? Did it rub salt in the wounds? Did you realize you're doing better than you thought you were? Did it make you realize that narcissism may exist in your business?

This is where the rubber meets the road.

We can't allow our need for sales to cause us to vomit our business on our people.

If you're not careful, you'll not only miss sales opportunities, but you'll rob yourself of dozens of referrals.

Here's a simple hack that I use...

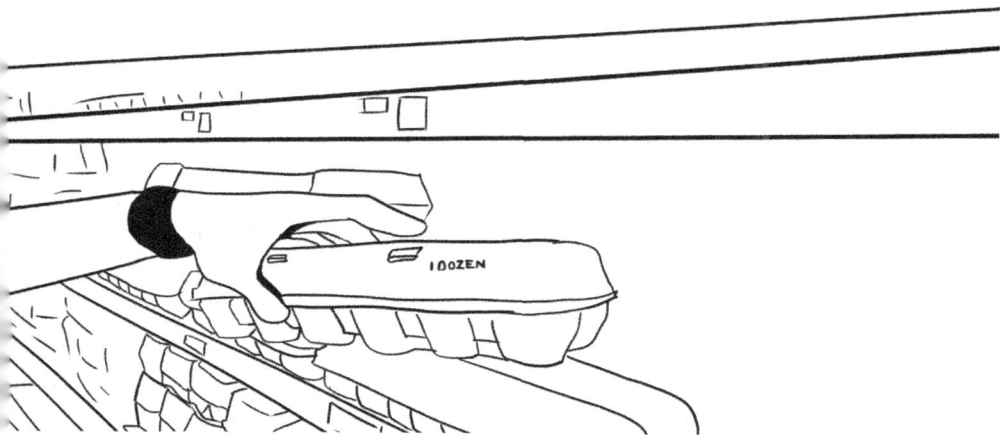

I've trained myself to see social media as an incubator for referrals instead of a farmers' market for sales.

That's not why your friends are there. They are there to get away from life. They are there to be entertained. They are there to be educated. They are there to feel lifted up and better about themselves. They aren't there for your record sales month or your next "Black Friday Deal."

If you want to be trusted, you'd better be better!

How do we get people to trust us more?

Stop introducing yourself. We introduce ourselves to strangers. So, when you do that in your videos, your friends think you're a fool. Jump directly into your content. You don't have time to waste anyway. By the time your intro is over, people are already swiping past your video.

Add genuine value to their life. When I create content that doesn't ask for business but helps someone learn and grow, they instantly trust me more. Stop being a walking billboard and come from a place of value.

Tell stories. Most business people just post data, numbers, and accolades. They don't tell stories. Stories help others relate to you. Stories help others see themselves in your story. Stories are entertaining. Great storytellers are typically trusted by others.

Be the same person in different situations. If who you are in public and in private aren't the same, you'll always struggle with social media.

When I travel and speak, it makes my heart so happy to hear people say that I'm exactly how they thought I'd be in person after watching my videos. I love it!

Can people say that about you? If you're a walking contradiction, you're going to have a hard time building a real rapport with people.

The bonus to being trustworthy is this...you'll get referred way more than you do now.

I don't give referrals to certain people because I don't truly trust how they'll treat the people I would refer to them. My reputation is on the line every time I send a referral out. Take that seriously. If you do, it will change the perspective you have of how social media works.

To-Do: If you realize you've been super salesy on social media. If you have been making your social media all about you, I want you to jump on video today or at least make a post apologizing to your people. Tell them that you have been reading a book that is blowing your mind (maybe the book isn't that good, but you can't be mad at me for trying, right? Ha.) and you are going to do social media differently moving forward.

Apologize for being selfish. Apologize for being all about yourself. Promise to start adding more value and being more yourself. Your people will eat it up! This will be huge for you if you do!

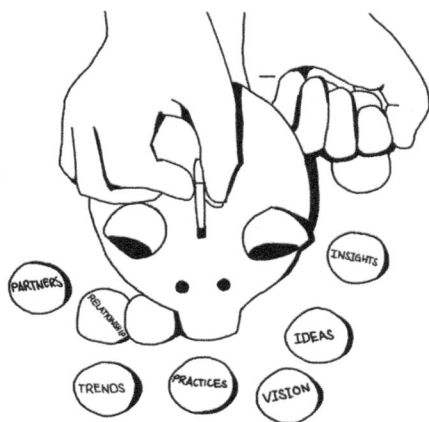

CHAPTER 8:
Relational currency

Growing up, my parents did a great job of not only teaching me but modeling for me that every single person matters. They were always giving people money. Taking meals to the homes of families in need. In high school and middle school, we were always the house that had 10-20 teenagers in it. They just loved serving people.

And you know the quote…

"The harder I work the luckier I get."

I watched opportunity after opportunity happen for my parents because they served people well.

I watched them grow a great business on the backbone of loving people.

They taught me the compounding effect of relational currency.

In business, we like to talk about win-win opportunities and how great it is when that happens. But in my world, I just want you to win. I do my best to leave my self-interests out of it.

It keeps me honest. It allows me to actually listen and not just sell you something because it's my job, but determine if what I sell is even right for you.

I have learned that if after every conversation the other person leaves the winner, I win a lot too! Here's a good exercise to think about…

Exercise: When was the last time you told someone no? I mean, they wanted your product or service, but after hearing their story, you just knew it wasn't the right fit or they weren't ready for it?

Really think about it. If you aren't telling anyone no, you don't care about people as much as you think you do.

Everyone isn't the right fit for your product or service. When I tell people no, it creates relational currency. They instantly are shocked that a sales guy put his benefit aside for theirs.

And most of the time, that same person will come back later and sign up or they'll refer me to someone who does. Relational currency is powerful stuff!

Now, we don't just earn relational currency by saying no, we also earn in all the moments that we simply put others first.

When I create genuine content that serves others, I'm stacking up "relational currency."

When I take an hour-long call with someone that isn't going to be a client but needs my help, I'm stacking up "relational currency."

When I speak at an event and talk to someone for 20 minutes about what they are struggling with, that's relational currency.

Wednesday of this week an appointment hit my calendar with a person I hadn't spoken to in a long time. We jumped on a call and she needed coaching and wasn't ready to pay for my content creation service, but I let her book another call with me anyways. She wanted to start a podcast, but it was obvious she wasn't sure where to start and I decided to serve her anyways.

That is building relational currency.

Get involved in a non-profit. Serve at your church. Tell the neighbors you'll watch their kids so they can have a date night. Stand at the gas station and hold the door open for 10 people. Make videos that aren't about you. Make serving people your priority.

I call it God, you might call it the universe, but at the end of the day, I reap what I sow and you might experience karma. It's the same ending…we get out of life what we give to it!

Side tip for married couples…stop keeping score and go outserve your spouse! Want to divorce-proof your marriage? Outserve your spouse without expecting a return! It will blow your spouse's mind!

Before we end this chapter, here are a couple of super practical social media examples of building relational currency…

#1 - DM three people every day and tell them you're thinking about them or praying for them (you better actually pray if you pick this one, ha). No strings attached.

#2 - When you see someone post about a birthday or anniversary, instead of posting on their wall or commenting, send them a video through DM instead. Get relational!

#3 - Take good notes on future transactions and check in months later with past clients. Ask how their daughter's soccer season is going. Check-in on their trip to Disney. Pick a detail that they shared and go deep into it. They will be shocked (in a good way)!

#4 - Do a pop-by social media style! If/when you see a friend of yours has a sick kid, go put a get-well kit together at CVS and drop it by their house. Then send them a DM telling them about it. This isn't rocket science guys, just be a GOOD PERSON!

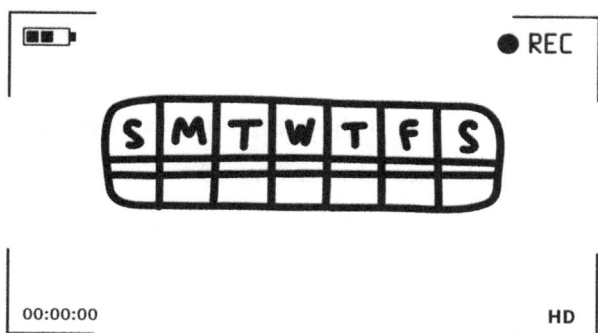

CHAPTER 9:
Daily Video!

I love The Rock! There, I said it.

I've seen all his movies multiple times, watched all his wrestling matches, and have seen all of his interviews on any talk show he's ever been on.

In my mind, The Rock and I should be best friends and if he walked into the Starbucks I'm writing in right now, I'd lose my mind. Ha.

Why?

This phrase was created decades ago for the one-way relationship between normal people and celebrities. We all have our favorite actors, comedians, talk show hosts, athletes, etc. If they walked into where you are reading this book right now, you'd freak out and they would have to be nice because of this whole para-social relationship thing.

This should matter to you because now we can have these types of relationships with other normal people.

Our brains don't quite know how to process the difference between when we are in-person with someone and when we see them on Zoom or our social media feed.

So, when you start doing video enough, your people will feel like they know you better and better. You'll get recognized in public. And most importantly, you'll be building trust with 100's of people because of para-social relationships!

This is why WE HAVE TO BE ON VIDEO EVERY DAY! (sorry I used all caps, but this is important)

Now, you don't have to post a public video every day. But you should be posting a video at least once a week (minimum) and then showing up daily in one-on-one opportunities.

This combination is where the power lies!

How do we do this? It's very straightforward...

Birthday Videos: Stop writing on people's walls on their birthdays and send them a video privately instead. And DO NOT automate this. Record them each day and say their name. Otherwise, they'll know it's fake. A friend of mine in Illinois sold 5 homes last year directly from birthday videos! How cool is that?!

Share Articles: As you read and learn, share interesting articles with a few friends that you think will be interested in them as well. Then send them a quick video telling them why you sent it to them, ask them for their opinion of it, then possibly even request to talk about it over coffee. Super simple.

Stop Window Shopping: We are all guilty of window shopping on social media. We look at pictures and watch videos, have thoughts about the people we see, but then don't say anything. Well, start saying stuff! If you see that your friends' 5-year-old just graduated from kindergarten, send them a quick video congratulating them, it goes so far!

In Your Processes: Look at your typical transaction. How often do you communicate with your clients? Three times? Seven times? Instead of doing that through text, email, or even a phone call, use video instead. Some of these videos will be able to be "evergreen" which means you can use them for all future clients. Others can be personalized. The power of your people seeing you on camera time and time again will position you to get so many referral opportunities. They need to see you and feel your energy, your passion, and your heart. Give it to them and watch them show up for you in the future!

I could go on and on about different ways to show up every day, but with just these few, you'll be well on your way to being remembered and valued far beyond the transaction!

CHAPTER 10:
You can't Give
what You Don't Have

If you want to create more value for others on social media, you better fill your cup!

Because it's hard. It's exhausting. It feels like a one-way street sometimes. It is lots of giving and way less receiving at times. But…but…but…it's worth it.

So, if you're going to change your approach to social media, you can't give what you don't have!

You can't pretend to have joy online, you have to actually have joy in your life.

You can't pretend to be full of energy on social media, you have to actually find energy in your life.

You can't teach people things on video if you aren't spending time learning yourself.

As I am almost a decade into my video journey...I've learned quite a few things about pouring into myself so I can pour into others.

#1 - Don't give to strangers until your family is getting the best of you.

I've been super guilty in the past of pouring my heart and soul into everyone around me and then being so tired at the end of the day that my wife and kids get the scraps. Protect and serve them first. I'm always trying to be better about putting my phone in the bedroom to be more attentive to the kids. I do my best to ask Lana questions about her day to help us stay connected. Lana and I also go to counseling together. Not because our marriage is bad, but because it's awesome and we want to keep it that way! Don't fall into the trap that many have and grow a great business only to lose your family. In my opinion, it's not worth it. Ever.

#2 - Allow fewer people into your circle.

In the past, it was so easy to let the wrong people's opinions matter the most. Some keyboard warrior would say something rude on social media and it would take me out for a couple of days. I've had to learn how to shut them out and pull the right people closer. I like to have a balance of three groups. People ahead of me know things I don't. People run at the same pace as me so we can learn and grow together. And people coming behind me so that I can help along their journey. If you're the smartest person in the room, you're in trouble!

The question I have gotten better at asking is, "What is true in what they said?"

When you seek out the truth, you don't knee-jerk as much. If there's truth in the criticism someone gave me, I have to have enough humility to receive it and get better. But whatever was based on just being harsh, it holds zero weight. Let it go.

Eat the fish and spit out the bones!

#3 - Read something every single day.

Our brain is so crazy...the moment we stop feeding it things that challenge it, it goes so dormant. When I struggle to create content and have low energy, it's almost 100% of the time related to my own personal development. The more new content you take in, the more you'll have to give away. The key to this is...as you LEARN, TEACH! This is the easiest content to make. Be a walking CliffsNotes for your people. Most of them will never read/watch/listen to what you do. So, give them the goods! They'll keep you around because of it.

#4 - Be grateful early.

We are human beings, which means we suck sometimes. If you aren't careful, you'll wake up, jump on social media, see someone doing better than you, and your day is shot. You're not doing a video now. So, get grateful early! Pray, journal, and do something for someone else. When I start my day with gratitude, it makes it a heck of a lot easier to get in front of the camera and put the needs of others before myself.

#5 - Do something for someone else.

It's hard to have a bad day when we do things for other people. There are studies that show that when we serve other people, we tend to just be happier. Buy the car behind you their coffee. Compliment someone. Send a nice text to a friend.

Give $20 to a homeless person on the corner. Just go out of your way, whether big or small, to help someone.

#6 - Assume the best in other people.

You cannot show up on social media the way you want if you're constantly mad or frustrated with someone. So, guess what? That person wasn't staring at you. They didn't cut you off on purpose. The tone your boss just gave you was an accident. Your wife didn't mean it.

Stop looking to be offended all the time! Stop it!

People aren't out to get you, they are too busy doing what's best for themselves.

The day you stop getting offended will be the day your social media changes forever!

#7 - Be a leader!

This is the most important one, that's why it's last! You are a leader. You are set apart. The fact that you're reading this book makes you value the right things more than most people. If you haven't noticed, our world is a rough place. Everyone is out for their own benefit. In my opinion, what would turn our world around? It's leadership!

People that want to get out in front of people and say, "Follow me!" I may not know everything, but I know how to serve and love people! Do you want to stand out on social media?

Go lead. You'll get noticed quickly!

YOUR PEOPLE
ALREADY KNOW
WHO YOU ARE

CHAPTER 11:
They Know Who You Are
(Do you?)

As this book moves into the 4th quarter (football reference), it's so important for you to remember that most likely, you've been taught how to do social media completely wrong.

You've been taught to make it all about yourself. To post your successes. Don't forget to tell people how great you are all the time.

I remember years ago being in a room full of top-producing Realtors and listening to someone stand in front of them (that they paid a lot of money for) and say, "If you don't remind people what you do every week, they'll forget."

It's all wrong! Do you know why?

Your people know who you are!!!!!!!

They know you're in real estate, they know you sell cars, they know you own an insurance agency, they know!

They don't forget what you do, they forget that you even exist!

You don't need to use your social media to continually remind them about what you do for a living…but instead, showcase your humanity, be relatable, and let them see the expertise you're bringing to the table.

One of your greatest takeaways from this book should be this…

Learn Passive Branding.

What is Passive Branding?

Passive Branding is talking about one thing while reminding people (without words) of another.

Let me break this down...

Ex. 1 - If you are sitting in the carpool line waiting to pick up the kids, do a video about a tip from your business or what the latest reports mean that came out about your industry.

This video won't feel "salesy" because it's coming from a personal environment. But it will be highly educational which will keep people paying attention.

Ex. 2 - Do a video about the webinar you just attended while you're sitting in your office.

This allows you to remind people about your business without having to say anything, but you're adding value because of the webinar you watched.

Ex. 3 - Do an educational video from your back porch where one of your kids could come out and "be a distraction."

The reason I put "be a distraction" in quotations is that you should welcome distractions like these. Most people would shut the camera off and start over, but not you, not anymore! You're going to come out of business character and be a dad/mom for a moment. Love your kid, tell them to say hi to everyone, then kick them off your porch and finish strong!

In one swoop, you were an expert, a loving parent, a funny parent when you kicked them out, then back to being an expert.

That is Passive Branding at its finest!

Early last year, as my speaking career started to pick up, I found myself in a big training room, about to speak to a room full of Realtors, and I was wearing a sports coat.

Well, if you're new to me, that's a big deal because I hate to dress up, it's just not my jam. I have a black suit jacket for weddings and funerals.

I did a great job at that event, but as I was heading home, I was looking at pictures and videos I'd been tagged in and I didn't even recognize myself.

I had allowed myself to be convinced that if I was going to make it as a speaker, I had to dress and look a certain way...and I believed it.

After seeing those pictures, I decided that I wasn't compromising who I am anymore. I started dressing how I want to dress (which is still very fashionable, ha), and guess what? My speaking career kept going up and I was able to keep charging more money.

The way I presented at events got even better. Why? Because I was being myself!

Don't miss this…if being yourself means wearing a power suit, that's awesome! Be you!

Don't let anyone tell you what you have to be to find success in your industry!

Find the right people that vibe with who you are, and you'll be blown away by the results.

Why does this matter?

It matters because doing social media is hard. But doing social media trying to be someone else is impossible.

Want to ruin your momentum before you even have any? Start doing social media as any version other than yourself.

If this is going to work for you, you have to be yourself. If we have 24 hours in a day, but you spend 8 hours sleeping and 14 hours performing for those around you, you're not leaving yourself very much time to knock out some content!

When you are yourself, you can hit that record button 24 hours a day.

☑ YOU ALREADY KNOW
WHAT TO DO

☐ _____

☐ _____

☐ _____

YOU ARE THE X-FACTOR!

CHAPTER 12:
You're The X-Factor

Can I be completely honest with you?

You don't need this book. You don't need any book for that matter.

Why?

Because you already know what to do. You know that social media and being in front of the camera is important. You know that your online presence matters. You know your industry is changing.

You're afraid to mess up. You're afraid to look stupid. You're afraid of what your sister is going to think? You don't know how to explain to your spouse and kids why you need to do videos and take more pictures when y'all are out and about.

You're choosing to bury your head in the sand to avoid the unknown…

No matter how hard you wish and pray…your industry is changing.

The way we communicate is shifting.

The way we get people's attention is different

Having to care about what we look like online is annoying…but no less true!

Do you want this book (or any book for that matter) to make a difference in your life and business?

Go be different than you've been before!

You are the x-factor!

What's the definition of insanity? Doing the same thing over and over again expecting different results

Be honest with yourself, have you given your best effort to social media?

Have you kind of farted around, it hasn't worked, and you've already said, "See, it just doesn't work for me."

Let's go! You are better than this! The fact that you're reading this book already makes you better than most!

You serve in an industry with plenty of shady people…and every day you put this off, you are leaving your people to fall victim to the wolves.

Take that spoonful of truth…

You're being so selfish, you're hiding behind your own insecurities to protect yourself.

Do you care about people or not?
Do you want the best for others or not?
Do you talk about how much you love helping people?

It's all bullcrap if you're not willing to do the hard things to make it happen!

So what do you say?

Everything we try that's new is going to be hard. You've overcome plenty of hard things in your life. What's one more?

Exercise: Before you read the last chapter (and it's special), stop right now, open up your camera, and start talking. You don't have to post it. Just practice.

Your business and the people around you will be so glad you did! Maybe, just maybe, tell people about this book! :)

CHAPTER 13:

My Secret Weapon

I love Jesus!

Now, hear me out…

If someone told me they had a secret weapon, I'd be super skeptical, but I'd also feel like an idiot if I didn't at least listen. So, just listen.

As many of you know, before I got into all this social media stuff, I was a youth pastor for about 9 years.

I worked with kids from 5th-12th grade, I led a college ministry, I worked with married couples, men's groups, and more.

I chose to go into ministry because God literally told me to.

I left church ministry because God told me to.

God told me to go be a businessman with the heart of a pastor...and here we are!

Why can I be so bold about my secret weapon that I am writing a whole chapter about it?

Because in a world full of hate, judgment, selfishness, lying, slander, malice, and plenty of other negative things, feelings, and actions...

- My relationship with Jesus keeps me centered.
- My relationship with Jesus gives me hope.
- My relationship with Jesus provides me with purpose.
- My relationship with Jesus helps me put others first.
- My relationship with Jesus grounds me in humility.
- My relationship with Jesus shows me a road map to serving people.
- My relationship with Jesus helps me love my family unconditionally.
- My relationship with Jesus keeps me from putting too much pressure on other humans.

- My relationship with Jesus allows me to give others the benefit of the doubt.
- My relationship with Jesus gives me the strength to shoot videos when I feel insecure.
- My relationship with Jesus reminds me I don't need the approval of others.
- My relationship with Jesus assures me that when I die, I'll spend eternity with Him in Heaven.

In my life, I've had many conversations with people who would call themselves, atheists.

They are some of my favorite conversations. I am so intrigued by how they come to the beliefs they have. My goal is never to "win," but my goal is to actually listen.

I want them to know that I love them. And I can't accomplish that by telling them they are wrong, I accomplish that by maybe being the first Christian they've ever met to actually listen to them.

No judgment. No condemning. *Just love.*

After listening to them for the majority of the conversation, I simply say this…

A lot of what you're saying makes sense. A lot of what you're saying I agree with.

But _____ (put your name there), I love casinos. I love gambling. I love playing the odds. I know I have a chance to win and a chance to lose. It gets my heart pumping.

There are some things though that I am not willing to chance…and where I spend eternity is one of them.

If you're right, and there is no God, there is no heaven, we simply get put in a box at the end of our lives…my life was still better because of my beliefs.

Our church helped raise our children to be upstanding humans. The Bible taught me my worldview. Helped me love others. It helped me sacrifice for those in need. Gave me a whole book to help me live a better life. I still feel like I come out on top.

But, if I'm right… there is a God that created this universe. And that same God gave His only Son to come down and live a sinless life, to die a sacrificial death, so he could resurrect 3 days later because He loved you so much. And if that means there is also a very real heaven and a very real hell, I want to end up in the right place.

And if that same man says that there is a life you can live that you can't even imagine if you'll simply ask Him into your heart...to me, that's a risk worth taking!

I know there are a lot of so-called Christians out there that give people like me a bad name.
I know there are a lot of so-called Christians out there that care more about your mistakes than their own.
I know there are a lot of so-called Christians out there that make you hate God.

But I beg you to consider this...

Stop judging a perfect God based on a bunch of imperfect people.

If you're not vibing with this, that's okay. Thank you, from the bottom of my heart for listening.

But if you're feeling some tugs on your heart right now...scan the QR code, I've got a video I want you to see.

This…is my *secret weapon*.

I tell myself everywhere I go, that my secret weapon is that I love helping others more than I care about looking stupid. What that really means is this…

God gives me everything I need. Through Jesus I have confidence, and acceptance, I'm loved, I'm forgiven, and I'm free. It is those things that allow me to not care what you think about me.

Because God already told me how proud He is of me.

In my opinion, this is the greatest advantage on the planet!

YOUR MINDSET IS EVERYTHING.

The way you see Social Media will be the way it is. Social Media will give you back what you put in. My last gift to you is this...my Social Media Affirmations! Say one of these out loud every morning. Repeat it over and over. Your people need you! Your people value your opinion.

Go be present in front of them...this is the simple difference between winning and losing online.

Made in the USA
Middletown, DE
18 September 2024

61105690R00057